TRACTORS
AND FARM MACHINERY

BY M. KAYE DAVID

STEAM BOOKWORKS

Note to Parents & Teachers

Steam Bookworks specializes in children's books focusing on **STEM (Science, Technology, Engineering, and Mathematics)** education topics while supporting literacy development.

This fun and engaging book uses effective teaching methods combining informational text, rhymes, wordplay, colorful layouts, dynamic photos, and glossaries. This book is designed to help children build vocabulary, become familiar with STEM concepts, and encourage reading success while appealing to their natural interests, imagination, and sense of play.

Suggested Activities

- Page through the book and look at the photos. Let the child respond to what they see. Ask questions.

- Review the highlighted vocabulary words in red. You can prompt the child by asking them if they know what it means. For example, *"Do you know what a 'cab' is?"* or *"Do you know what a 'hitch' is?"* or *"What do you think a hay baler does?"*

- Review the visual glossary, vocabulary list and definitions.

- Read the book to the child, or have them read it on their own.

- Discuss the book. You can prompt the child with questions:

  Have you ever seen a tractor?

  Have you ever been to a farm?

  Would you like to visit a farm?

  Where does our food come from?

  What do farmers do?

  What is a farm implement?

  Which one is your favorite machine? Why?

Copyright © 2021 Steam Bookworks. All rights reserved. No part of this book may be reproduced in any form without written permission from the publisher.

Table of Contents

Tractor Cab 10

Tractor Fuel 14

Plows 16

Harrows 17

Fertilizers 18

Combines 19

Mowers 20

Rakes 21

Balers 22

Bale Spears 23

Steam Tractors 30

Drones 31

Agricultural Technology 32

Visual Glossary 34

Vocabulary 36

Equipped with powerful engines and big, chunky tires, tractors have many qualities to admire.

They have plenty of **torque** to pull things along, slowly, surely, reliably, and strong.

They excel at hard tasks, hauling big, heavy loads,

and although they are slow, they can go on the road.

They can pull farm equipment, mow grass, and dig ditches,

by attaching **implements** to rear three-point **hitches.**

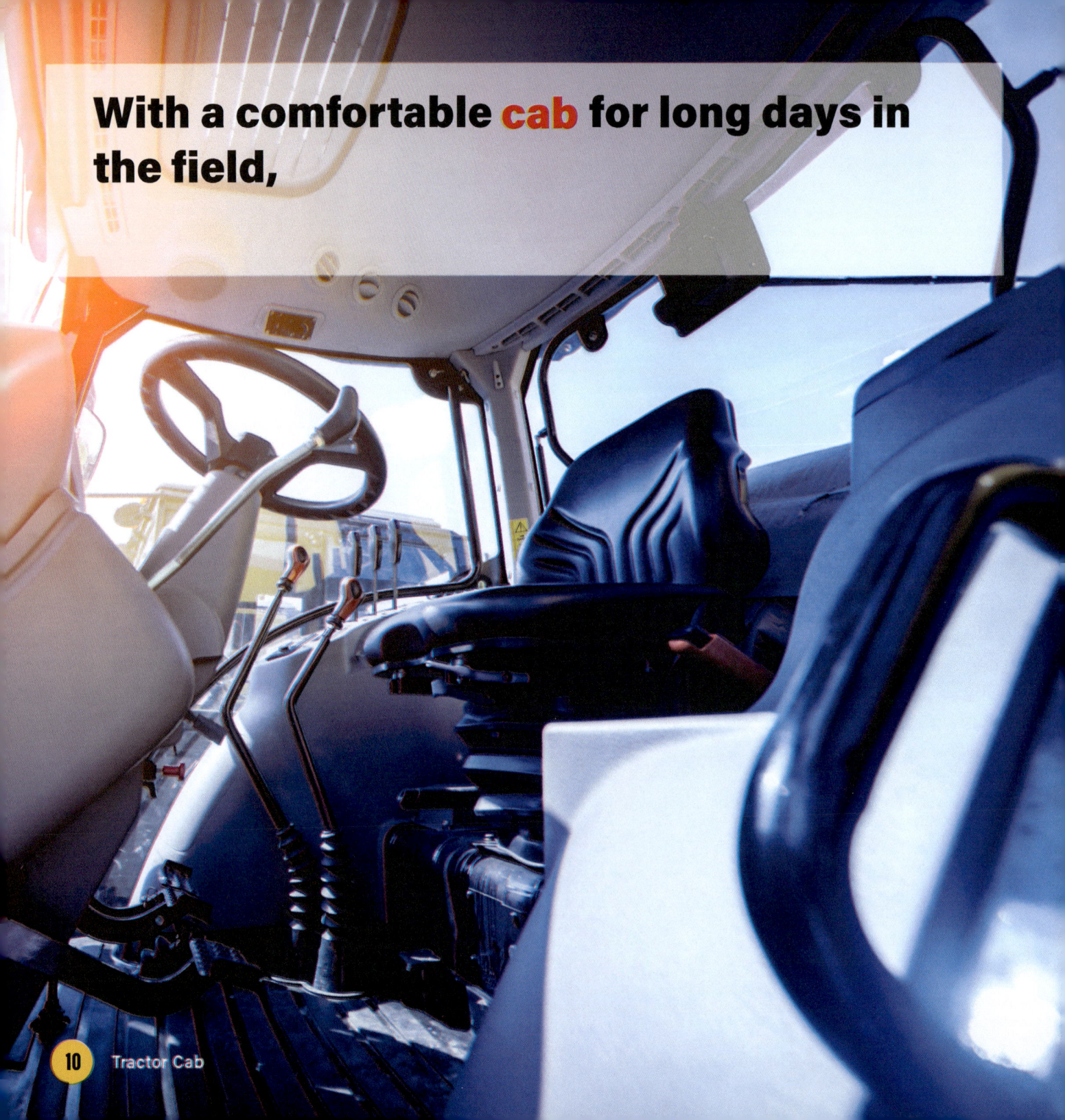

With a comfortable cab for long days in the field,

Tractor Cab

tractors can help farmers multiply their yield.

The glass-enclosed cab helps to see all around,

it does double-duty to block noise and sound.

Diesel is the fuel of choice in the tank, it powers engines right up like an energy bank.

14 Tractor Fuel

Now let's take a look at equipment in the field, when a farmer is taking a turn at the wheel.

Plows dig into soil preparing to **sow**, cutting and turning earth into **furrows**.

Harrows prepare soil for seeding—loosening, aerating, clearing, and weeding.

Harrows

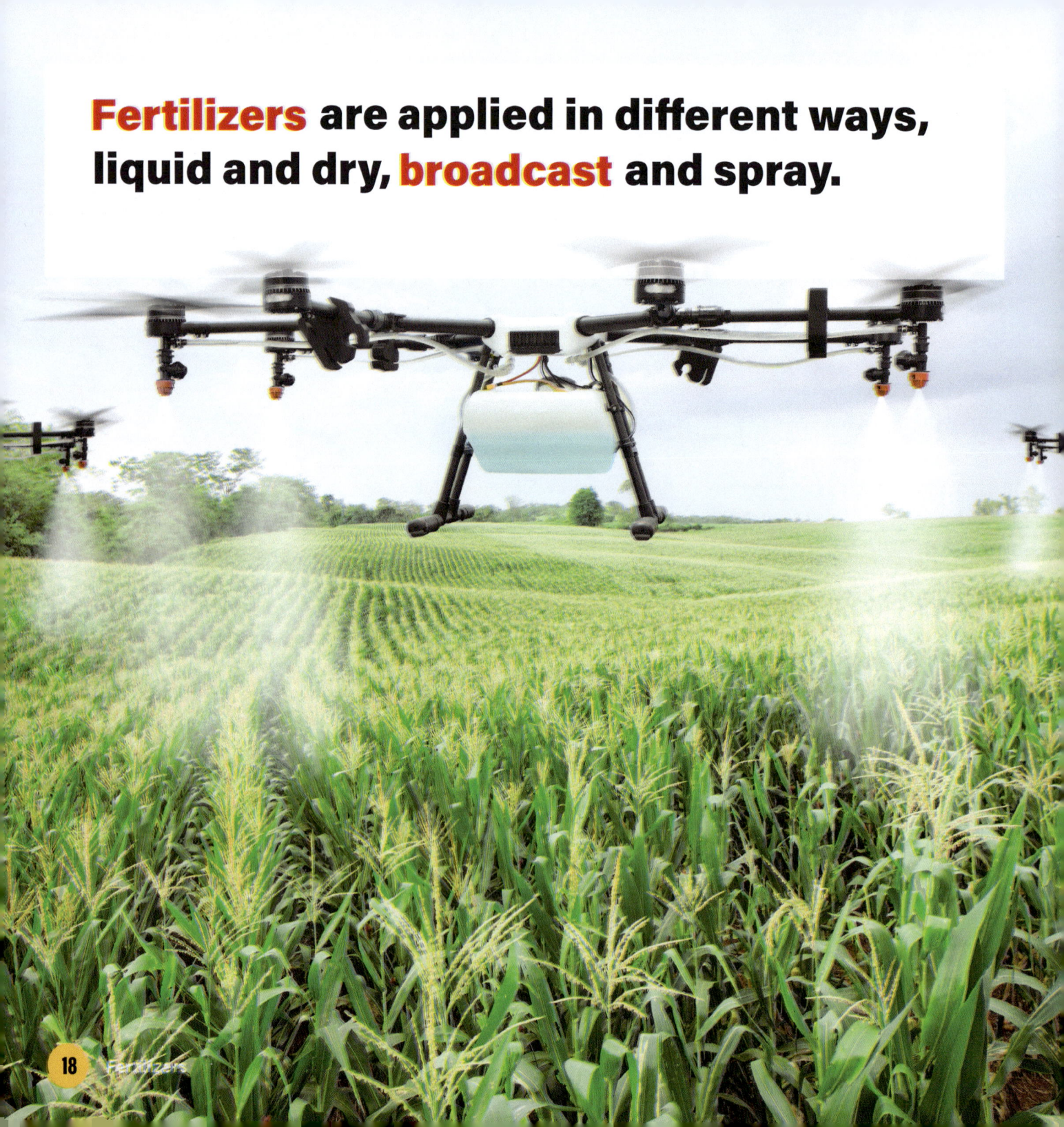

Fertilizers are applied in different ways, liquid and dry, **broadcast** and spray.

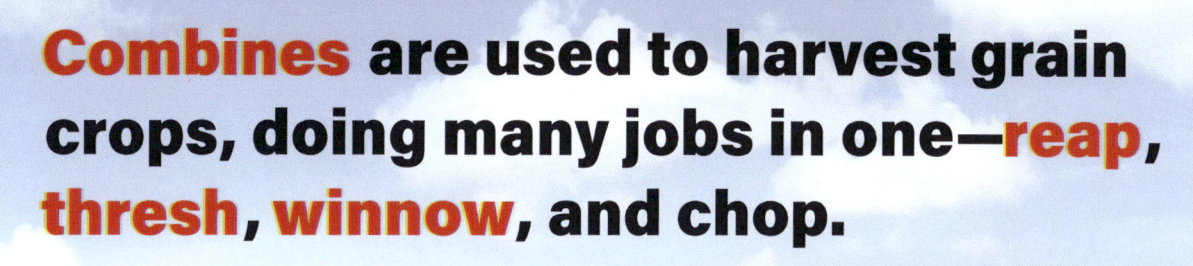

Combines are used to harvest grain crops, doing many jobs in one—**reap**, **thresh**, **winnow**, and chop.

Mowing and tedding are part of hay making.

To form the windrows, the tractor has to start raking.

Rakes 21

Balers roll up the hay, dropping them out from the rear.

The tractor loads them onto a truck with a spear.

Bale Spears

Bringing food to the table is what farmers do best.

They cultivate, plant, grow and harvest.

There are many decisions for a farmer to make,

from what seeds to plant, to which crops to rotate.

It takes great skill to manage a farm operation—planning, logistics, and organization.

From day into night, farmers work on the land using specialized machinery to lend them a hand.

Agricultural machines have a history of innovation,

Steam Tractors

from steam-powered engines to drone **navigation**.

Drones

From tilling, to sowing, to hauling, to mowing,

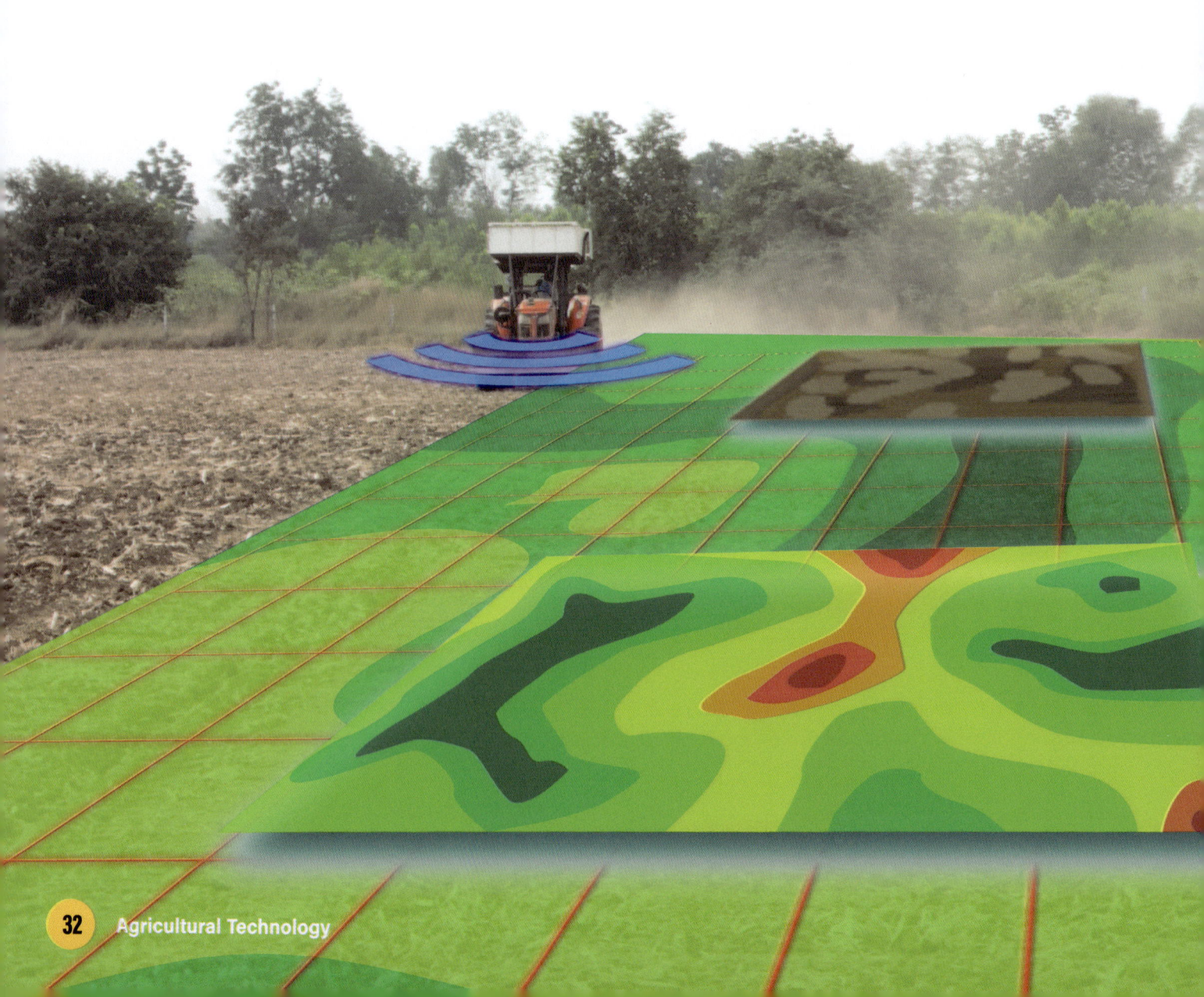

Agricultural Technology

engineering and science help with all that is growing.

These mechanical wonders can work without rest.

Tractor

Combine Harvester

Disk Harrow

Which one would you like to put to the test?

Drone

Moldboard Plow

Hay Baler

Vocabulary

baler
a machine that compresses and binds a crop such as hay and bundles it into rectangular or cylindrical forms for easier handling, transportation, and storage.

broadcast
to scatter material by hand or with a machine over a large area

cab
compartment of a truck or tractor where the driver sits

combine
machine designed to harvest grain crops such as wheat, oats, rye, and barley and combin the process of reaping, threshing, and winnowing

diesel
liquid fuel used in diesel engines in which the ignition results from compression rather than from a spark (as with gasoline engines)

fertilizer
organic or inorganic substance added to a growing medium that provides nutrients to plants to help them grow more productively

furrow
shallow trench or groove plowed into the soil to plant rows of seeds or seedlings

harrow
farm implement with a variety of blades and cutting edges to loosen soil, remove rocks and weeds, and prepare the soil for seeding

hitch
type of connector that can attach implements to a tractor

implement
piece of equipment designed to perform a task such as plowing, spreading fertilizer, or sowing seed

logistics
coordination and management of a complex process navigation

navigation
means of determining a position and planning a route

plow (or plough)
farming implement that prepares the soil for planting by cutting into and turning it over

reap
cut grain stalks

sow
plant the seeds of a plant or crop

tedding
fluffing hay to help dry it out

thresh
separate grain from the stalk

till
prepare soil for planting through various methods including digging, stirring and turning over; plowing and harrowing are examples of tillage

torque
the amount of rotational or twisting force to cause an object, like an engine's crankshaft, to rotate around an axis

windrow
hay that has been mowed, tedded, and raked into a row and left to dry, with the help of sun and wind

winnow
separate grain from the chaff

yield
measure of the amount of crop or product that has been grown, harvested, or produced

Printed in Great Britain
by Amazon